HOURS

By Frances Mayes

Frances Mayes

HOURS

LOST ROADS
Number 23 1984
Providence, Rhode Island

Grateful acknowledgment is made to the following publications in which these poems first appeared: *Coastlight, Five Fingers, Review, The Little Magazine, Ploughshares.*

"22 Ointments Against The Hand Of A Ghost" was printed as a broadside by Rebus Press, Berkeley, California, for Stanford University's conference "Women Writing Poetry in America."

Library of Congress Cataloging in Publication Data

Mayes, Frances.
    Hours.

    (Lost roads ; no. 23)
    I. Title. II. Series.
PS3563.A956H6 1983   811'.54   82-84379
ISBN 0-918786-26-6

Notes

The quotes in "A Quipu Knot For Arguedas" are from *Deep Rivers*, (Los Rios Profundos), by José Maria Arguedas, translated by Frances Horning Barraclough, University of Texas Pan America Series, 1981.

The italicized fragments in "The Shadow Of Increase" are from several poems by Louise Bogan.

The line quoted in "December, Thunder Is In The Middle Of Earth" is by Wallace Stevens.

Published by Lost Roads Publishers
P.O. Box 5848 Weybosset Hill Sta.
Providence, Rhode Island 02903
First Printing by Industrial Impressions

Cover painting by H. Lane Smith
Book design by Forrest Gander and C.D. Wright

This project is supported by a grant from the National Endowment for the Arts in Washington, D.C., a federal agency.

CONTENTS

The boat came breasting out of the mist and in they stepped.
All new things in life were meant to come like that.

Eudora Welty

LOOK AND SEE

Luscious the world of solid objects, shorn wool, thyme,
starfish, close rows of turnip tops. The optical truth:

My distinct body gaining on my shadow as I run. Between
the dermis and epidermis, a layer of pure energy. Horses

Cantering the ring, pointed bills of stilts, the cleft
in the cat's nose, see: tiny ram's horns or the letter Y.

Tap shoes are made to tap. And lips: those lips the gods
would like to touch with theirs if there were gods. Classic,

Skipping body, wholly here and blooming sure as a tiger
lily. The act of actually flying in hard air, thrown to

The floor of the sky, whispering to the miscellaneous
constellations. Cycles of dawn engender clichés and tragedy,

Unlikely as dirigibles. Heaven to me, is a Japanese garden
of sand raked in patterns, not the night my tooth crumbled

In the restaurant. No ambiguity there. Just the constant
concept of choice, always the danger that this is the last

Gift before parting forever. A pearl, lying on a bed of cotton,
restlessly symbolic. Take the ugly cactus pear instead.

Pulled open is the taste of rose. The real, a finite fact
staining all the raw planks. If the sheaf of tissue is left

The whole rib grows back. An overgrown garden. Loaf of milk
bread. Dream of Queen Bess in brown skirts. Man in ski hat

Breaking in. Tighten the cello bow. Historical depth will
surface and plunge at random. I walk the long spine of
 San Francisco.

All faces remind me of someone, as if X hides in this or
that face. I'm weaving chains of St. Augustine grass.

Not experience, gathered into fascicles and tied with ribbon,
but the day as it is lived. The root of the clump is single.

Bizarre movement of maimed people parodies the maimed.
Hardly art for art's sake; a crippled man crossing the street

Is very crippled. The school of minnows flashing resembles
a galaxy, a handful of mica flung, only in the mind. In the eye,

Silver fish turn in clear water. His dark suit, her pure
peau de soie, various poses of the dance. Beneath, the molten

Body, its wax and gutters, lost gills, moles, articulations.
Mingled with the genuine, you must fill out a report. Split

A beer. Many thinkers have fired their carbines. Will someone
get a blanket? The nights are cool and just. The joyous world

Is as close as it will ever be. Striped umbrellas, salt breeze.
White moth on the screen, mothers, ruffled water. My feet bare

On the back of the horse. Knees slowly unbending, then up, arms
out for balance. We go. Vivacious, alert, and meaning explicit.

for William Dickey

FOLDING SHEETS

In the boneyard at night
they get up to iron.
The angels step off the crosses.
Always there's moonlight.
A white cat glinting like mica.
The mouths of the dead
are stuffed with cotton.
They are plain now. Light.
They dampen well and never scorch.

CHILDHOOD SCENE IN BARFIELD'S DRUG STORE

This begins with me, a child of eight.
Cool marble pharmacy lined with mirrors.
It's after ballet at Miss Ann's with fat thighs.
I'm not talking to Jane Floyd who's having Coke.
I'm kicking the cylinder of the stool.
A little fan nods right, left on its base.
It's way back. Only the smell of milk
bubbles in soda water and a thick straw
I'm bending. Then my Mother. She doesn't see
me. Glides in, asks for, does she say
Unguentine? and a lipstick, Fire and Ice.

Above the counter Dr. Barfield's
cantaloupe head, slit for lips.
He brings up little bottles. I see her
face in the mirror. She's dabbing
her wrist, her pearls swing, eyelids
down like a doll's. I'm in my hard body.
How can she *be* over there. In memory

There is a click, we each look in
opposite mirrors, her face in mine.
For a moment, no recognition.
I spin around then she crosses
over. Her checked dress and smile,
sound starts back, the black fan,
radio, Racing with the Moon. And it
ends under layers of time, after many
voices say, You have your Mother's eyes.

LETTER FROM THE WORLD

When the rain hits the window
I think of tent revivals in the South.
They'd sweep in town from nowhere,
taking over a field. This storm—
from Asia, blown fast over the Pacific.
Repent, repent. Stick figure
holding back the flap, beckoning.
The room breaks loose, drifts
through the city in fog.

Hard percussive strokes repeat.
Houses struggle to hold up their outlines.
Wind that could send
pine needles straight through panes.
O, eye of the beholder, fierce night.
Hands all over the city parting curtains,
watching out. The view is under
pressure. Tree that was tree
every day lies suddenly over
a yellow Pontiac. Crushed, uprooted,
dangling nerves. We are real. Are
solid. Cast shadows. Sweet faith,

We're safe inside, this is simply
a harder rain. I'm like Emily hidden
upstairs at the window, saw the circus
passing in the dark, saw Araby entire.
Red sirens pull my vision, careening
slick streets. Wind's inquisition,
starting rumors. We may not be spared.
Even the dead are soaked by now.
A careless god walking the roof.
His odor of ozone. The naturalness

Of random destruction, and the beauty
of the rest. I see the glass studded
with blue diamonds, scarf of fog
around the streetlight. Rain adds and
subtracts with abandon. To whom
it may concern. To whom it may
concern. I look for signs. Petals
of rain, hooves of rain, nails of rain.
A stray cat runs, electrified,
paws drumming the wet earth.

22 OINTMENTS AGAINST THE HAND OF A GHOST

‡ Spot a migrating tern in the clouds.

‡ Rub buttermilk into your breasts every evening.

‡ Paint the car nailpolish red.

‡ Remember this action is insignificant in itself.

‡ Pour a glass of brandy, lie on the floor in your
sleeping bag and play the tape of your grandmother's funeral.
When they come to "Jerusalem, Jerusalem," join in
the singing.

‡ Balms: formosa oolong, fennel seeds, Indio dates,
catalpa leaves.

‡ Dress the scarecrow as an archer.

‡ Place his ashes in an eggtimer so that he might still
be useful.

‡ After each loss, double the stakes.

‡ Wake slowly so your wandering spirit has time to find
your body.

‡ Write "La Vita Nuova" in three faultless Latin paragraphs.

‡ Identify the generating principles in terms which account
for the work's development.

‡ Sleep in a black blindfold.

‡ Write a chant to say on rising, beginning with Shine
a light, how far to London, put out the night, who is
the green-eyed man?

‡ Kiss the shoulders of a lyric poet.

‡ Burn the old clothes.

‡ Remember the Greyhound driver said, "After a certain
distance, it's $99 to anywhere."

‡ Cut up the letters that spell the ghost, make a dozen
new words.

‡ Wash your face in three kinds of water.

‡ Locate the constellation of your birth; give it a better
name.

‡ Imagine March 3, 2802, imagine the daffodils,
bedroom, horizon, then.

‡ Pace back and back along your sleeping mother's bed
until she opens her stone eyes and says, Heart, heart
heart, heart, heart.

SPELL AGAINST THE HAILSTORM IN FITZGERALD, GEORGIA

Think of your blind grandmother, blank
eyeballs of an angel looking to heaven.

Suck jawbreakers in the dark. Oh,
chicken little, all the sultry

Afternoon, play Ping-Pong on the porch.
Whose is the jar of gallstones?

Look, your graduation pearls unstrung,
mothballs melting in the folded seams.

Squeeze, gently, into your mouth
a soft turtle egg. Touch the cabinets'

Crystal knobs. All the faraway
moons of Jupiter are hitting the roof.

Your turn, your turn, you'll need snake eyes
to win when you roll those worn-down dice.

RED DIGITS READ 12:47

Three anemones in a glass.
I arrived on foot.
His house is empty.
My white sundress damp.
I fold my hands at the table,
admire the firm
statement of bloom.
Hot and late.
His house. His cut
nails in the ashtray.
I thought we would
stop only by death.
I'd be the one
to daub the boat
with pitch, shove his body
on fire to the waves.
Where's he now?
My dark sayings
came true. Silence
is a trumpet blast.
His fingerprints
are all over my body.
We were together
in the big times and
in throwaway moments.
The digits flip time

Over, squared, a red glow.
I turn into him. Alone
at home on a random night.
Wine and a stranger.
Or loneliness spreading
fast like a gas fire.
The seasons I've been gone

pull through me.
I've a spirit bare
from hard scrubbing.
I wish moths
were not eyelids on the lamp.
My blood is noisy.
A hand covers my mouth.
The porch light burns out.
I don't know

What I'm missing.
One bird singing
owns night
in this yard. I'm still
as a cup of salt.
Locking, unlocking.
But nothing disrupts
the severe order
of his shoes. Is it
over? His mirror,
size of one face.
Mine: animal eyes.
The blind woman inside me
pieces together
a black puzzle.
I pass the night
in such solitude.
Rain on leaves.
Like cures like.

LIKE WITTGENSTEIN'S LAST WORDS

Her life was running along with me.
And now that I have seen her backbone
and soft organs held to the light,
I'm waiting. She was never so intimate
of me. I was the one to get the three
dark cries. This is the Hoping Room
where people are floating down the margin
of blue chairs. Outside, wind. As good
a day as any. The clerk asking coffee,
anything. There's nothing but wonder.
Death is not a part of life.
In a dream, words wrote themselves
on a wall. Some were *bala, tet, ter,*
I cannot even recognize the language.
TELL THEM I'VE HAD A WONDERFUL LIFE.
She's sleek, a light imprint.
When in the future I am nostalgic
I may notice more. I dial the number
of a friend I know isn't home.
That morning I wrote down all the words
I remembered. They were from nowhere inside me.

THE OTHER EDGE OF JUNE

Someone is late, I'm waiting.
The hot smell of rain on the street
brings you close, now that you
are of little use and gone. Two
boys throw yellow and blue
balloons. Distended with water
they swag down the air, plop
into the boys' open hands.
This will be *summer* to them,
in Palo Alto in the eighties.
My grandfather born in the other
eighties. They will have this
vast oak over their childhood,
the golden retriever barking,
father moving out and the house
billowing with silence. Heat
ripples through my my feet, decades,
my grandfather tossing
on the ocean at five, scared,
a bag of apples in his fist,
his Aunt Lilly on shore watching
him recede in the spyglass,
waving to his white shirt.
Often I send you out as a boy
to run through the cotton fields
although I don't know why.
Her pink dress the last he'd
see of England. I should unravel
myself from your life by now.
They could fall from that shaky
treehouse. My grandfather landed
in time. A red car passes
so slowly, as if pulled
through green water. No one

is coming down the tunnel
of sycamores, someone is late.
Skinny boys with short shadows.
The rope to the treehouse
stings their palms and soles.
The day will soften, white
birch tops air-brushed
with gold. Here, these are
the eighties. The yellow
balloon stops in the air
long enough for me to wonder.
You take the corner
fast in another world.

IF THEN

It's a dicey countdown.
Still, I'm in the habit of living,
I volunteered for it.
Hello, what's your nickname now?
Most people are far back in themselves.
You like dogs and cats, who
inhabit their lives up front.
Your lips are sealed.
See, sad horse-brown eyes,
this is what comes of the years
of wearing hand-me-downs to weddings.
You saved my postcards, now
you're turning over in the grave,
needing the exercise. No
criticism intended. I've picked hairs
off the pillows too. I can sleep alone,
make a minus sign, learn to think
abstractly. I'm licking down that fur.
Whoever is tapping the water glass
with a spoon can stop now.
In the old, we poured prayers
into each other's ears.
In the new, I clap on more sail.
The mnemonic for compass correction is
Can Dead Men Vote Twice. True course
depends on an elegant solution.
You let me feel your iron hand.
You sink into me.
My brain smolders, oily rags.
You're outlined in black, filled
with bright color. A cluster bomb,
pomegranate, flies' eyes.
You drive everything into the ground.
The circuit is not adequate for the voltage.

Should I pull anchor or give it more rode.
A disadvantage for hairless bodies to shiver.
You took a deep breath before diving,
whistling to clear the blood.
Ready for the cold pack mud dark?
Now you're down to the basic layer
of English, where it meets the fiery shadow.
Pig snout, walk out, egg shell, inside out.
Three stops and run forever.
I look back and forth like someone at a tennis match.
You're just tired of your own rattle.
The cast off skin shows no color of the former owner.
The deeds are transferred.
I pour you back in the jug.
Silence will be pleased to hear this.

AUGUST, BY WATER

Key

On the first of August I woke up in my old room, a key turning in the back door.

There's Willie, I thought, it must be seven thirty.

For a moment I was deep in my white spool bed, the covers thrown back. The sleeping house stretched out around me. And Willie, Willie! was opening the door, about to start breakfast before anyone was up.

Then I was sharply awake, unsnagged from my mother's house. And someone opened the front door here in California, years later.

Willie was left on the top step, the key in her hand. I sat up suddenly, crowded with loss and relief.

Rain

In summer there is little water here except the ocean and it is bitter. Looking out at the empty blue dome of sky, I am thinking of Georgia, the air weighted in August. At two o'clock heat cracks the sky open. Lightning darts down so close you instinctively draw back. Then the sweet rain falls.

Just as quickly, it stops and the sun makes an angry comeback, pulling steam from the heated streets, wilting the dresses of old ladies who have risen from their naps, blistering the hurtful white sides of houses. The current of heat purrs in your body with only one relief.

The long black stream, glazed with silver like the sleeve of a wizard, numbs your feet. As you lower yourself into the water, you forget if you are hot or cold. At first, you seem to heat the water with your body, then the hard shock of cold, a flash freeze to the blood. With your feet you feel the sandy bottom until you find the cold springs, spurting pure as Easter water. You are so cold you were never hot before, you were always ice, always a body carved from quartz. Then you climb out in your cleanest skin, burning with cold.

500 Years

In the five hundred year old painting, a woman has removed her clothes in August. She sits on the bank of the Juine, about to go in the water. When I am that woman I am back on the edge of that stream where the atavistic rock fish swim up to hide in the black water. But she feels the Duke's chateau behind her. In the distance she sees the princess and her friends setting off with the falcons on their wrists. Her brothers already are in the water, their thick bodies freed, two tadpoles. Five hundred years or a day like this. It is a simple thing to drop one's blue dress in the grass. To sit still before entering the water. You know how you belong to yourself in such a moment. Looking at her, 500 years slide away. A river flowing backwards. I am resting there. All the past is equally over. In a moment she will slip into the current and become one with the brown and violet fish.

Dog Days

I asked Willie what that meant. "It means dogs go mad from the heat and run us up and down the streets, foaming at the mouth."

But that was in childhood on the sweltering back porch where the lattice cut the sun to bits. "This time of year, you better watch out." I was helping Willie shell peas into a brown bag, kept quiet while Mother and her friends played bridge in the dining room. We could hear the shuffling of cards and the click of ice in their tea glasses. Mother's friend Alicia was back home from Asheville where she went for shock treatments almost every August when the year got to be just too much. "Bull dogs are the worst. They sink those teeth in your leg and you'll never know what bit you."

Alicia never forgot a card, could bid baby slams and make them all the time; Mother said it had nothing to do with diamonds and hearts. When Willie and I took in the chilled

plates of pressed chicken and frozen fruit salad, I saw Alicia
looking at little rolls of paper she took out of her purse.
Willie told me she saw *Ginger, Robert,* the names of Alicia's
children, and *2908,* her own telephone number, her address
and where she was born. Willie said that was all. She said
the treatments are like reshuffling the cards after the hand.
She said if one bites you, you'll foam at the mouth too.

Vita

Think of the Pope in the earth with his white veil over his
face. Now that Sirius in the jaw of the dog is rising with
The sun, he is newly dead.
His feet in red shoes now point toward the resurrection.
He is ready, holding a paper inscribed with his
Accomplishments.
But it is only August.
The time of year you too would answer.

Vita, you write.
Urbi et orbi and the bridge club in a lonesome hot town
in the pine barrens.

Birth, schools, a few honors.
But you feel quickly the facts go false.
You turn facetious: I drove in Paris and did not avoid L'Etoile.
You pause, draw a ladder and a butterfly.
You forget what you started because it is so hot
And begin to list the groceries: mustard, eggs, peaches,
What *is* asked.

Soul

In August Emerson wrote in his journal: Last night a walk
to the river with Margaret, and saw the moon broken in
the water, interrogating, interrogating.

It is death to the soul to become water.
Heraclitus

This lake is flat, lit from inside like white jade.
You see your arms turn livid underwater, your feet
Grow solid as a fertility idol's.
When all is refracted
Let the soul be a swimming animal.
Let it scrape the bottom. Breathe
Water until it grows gills.
For water itself is perfectly water
And is without question.
When the body floats
Let the soul be flagrant and fishy.
For the soul knows no great dog in the heavens
And behind the stories you tell
The stars are as they are.
Let the soul dive for the lost herb,
Silvery and invisible.
For the soul is five hundred years old in August.
Let the body be buoyed
And the soul somersault.
For all the dreams of August pull you under.
Let the soul divine by water.
Let the cool mud settle
And this be called psalm.

Calling Marco

My friend wanders back from vacation saying, "I have been reading about the War of the Roses and I may get a divorce. There are many kinds of nirvana and all of them are expensive."

Looked at one way, there is much madness. Another, everything evens.

The Jehovah's Witnesses swarm the neighborhood. Their pamphlet says: The next time a playful puppy or kitten licks you or someone in your household, think: Is rabies prevalent in our area?

Is it? But the lawns are orderly. No charging bulldogs among the flowers blooming on cue. My dog won't even stand up for the Witness.

Time for the back to school dream.

Dog-day cicadas, a deeply end of summer sound from childhood. This is how night sounds when it breathes. All that is missing is the attic fan pulling in moist smells of the pine and hydrangea around my mother's house. Why do the cicadas sing together? I am twelve but I am not. My own child and her friend are splashing in the water with their eyes closed, calling   Marco   Polo
Marco   Polo

The Year Moves

like the wild tide
in the Bay of Fundy
a raised shelf of water
moving in too fast to level.

This is how you are riding
high over the months and years.
You feel them shifting under
you, cold and swift.

Last Hour

So the summer is to burn through my fingers
like so many others, like hundreds of others.
The hills are scorched gold,
so dry they beg a match.
No need to burn.
I forget I am reasonable
though it is so clear I can see
out to the islands, cut clean as puzzle pieces.
A warm wind rounds Mt. Tam.
I lie in the grass with a glass of wine.
I am waiting for the earth to turn the corner.

Because San Francisco and the lapis sea
are below us, someone says
Is this the most beautiful place in the world?
Then the sun just drops down into the water,
leaving us astonished,
lying quiet on the slope,
only the sound of the grass
parting around us.

SHOUTING SONG

No more listening to that sliding way of singing.
Pepper his tracks.
You long for the divine taste on your tongue.
Is that a smile or a slab of cold grits?
Raise the anchor or cut the ropes.
Your hair will not grow miraculously to conceal you.
He breathes either or either or either or.
There is no message hidden in the body of a hare.
Gertrude said the difference is spreading.
All the cradle songs just put the world to sleep.
You're no zoo seal taking violent turns in a tank.
Life is long, in a way.
Devote only ten minutes a day to remembering the past.
Snakes know: hook the skin at the mouth,
Peel off in one piece. Underneath, you're slick and thirsty.
You won't be waiting in a park at twilight at the end of the
      century.
Triple time will do.
If ever there is an apocalypse, it will be Flannery O'Connor
In the sky pulled in a chariot by peacocks.
Now, vote with your feet.

TEA OLIVE IS NOT IN THE DICTIONARY

Is that the right name for the tree that grew outside my bedroom window? The scent was airy, spicy, and I preferred it to the dizzy perfume of the gardenias and magnolias that ruled the neighborhood. To think of the origins of writing is to remember first impulses, first events, and their resonances.

A first memory is of my father. He and his hunting friends, Bascom and Royce, are drinking bourbon. From my room in the back of the house, right off the kitchen, I see through the keyhole (keyholes were a large part of my childhood) the pile of doves on the sink and someone's hand cleaning a shotgun barrel with a dishrag. When the friends go, my father still sits at the table with his tumbler of bourbon. I'm reading with a flashlight under the covers. My specialty is orphans on islands. The houses have trapdoors into secret passageways that lead to the sea. Rowboats, menace, treasure. As the water gets darker and the danger grows, I hear my father talking to himself. When I look out, I see his head in his hands, his blood stained coat hung on the back door. Very late, he hits the wall with his fist, and says over and over, "The beastly, Christly South, this beastly, Christly South." I put the palm of my hand over the spot where he is pounding with his fist and feel the vibration all the way up my arm.

At seven, there is little to make of such a happening. Years later, if the grapple hook of memory, in its search for explanations, raises the moment from the mud, perhaps it explains something.

Augurs in ancient times examined the dropping of animals, flight patterns of birds, and the alignments of stars. I have done much of that to understand my past, wants, and passions. Almost everything I assumed or was force-fed growing up in Georgia has been hauled in for questioning. I've thrown out several babies with the bath water, so to speak, and have spent more time than I *had* ferreting out my motives and whether certain acts are too masculine influenced, from the wrong hemisphere of my brain, or from the lady-belle tradition and therefore suspect.

Does the South, as a *place* for literature, still exist? Does a woman's sensibility, as form, exist? Or has the South been stereotyped beyond use; has the blatant affirmation of women's writing in the heyday of the feminist movement drifted back into a tradition only slightly altered by a vague androgyny? What interests me now is what's underneath the questions.

My South, the place I have no choice but to call home, is lonesome country where you can drive for miles without seeing more than a rattlesnake cross the road. At the city limits of town a sign says, If you lived here you'd be home now. The logic is, I suppose, irrefutable, though it leaves me with a slight sense of panic. Thin roads wavering in the heat lead into Fitzgerald from Ocilla, Mystic, Land's Crossing, and Irwinville, where Jefferson Davis was captured by the Yankees, dressed up like a woman, to his eternal shame. South Georgia— as beautiful as it is benighted. Clear springs to dive into, long leaf pines, racism in the marrow bone, the heat that makes your heart beat thickly against your chest, the grotesque self-satisfaction of those of us who have *always* lived there, the fine caring for each other. A place of continuous contradiction. This neck of the woods was called for a brief time, Carter country, although my mother maintains yet that she never heard of any Carters. I think, of course, of Flannery O'Connor and Carson McCullers, and, more recently, of Alice Walker, from the same swath of earth. If writing comes partly out of a cultural tension, always present in the South, it is interesting that women writers have sprung up in this small area. With the exception of Conrad Aiken, born up in Savannah, I think no man of this region has been heard of in literature since Sidney Lanier wore assonance and consonance out forever. Although our times are not exactly the same, I imagine Carson over in Columbus, Flannery (raising a chicken that walked backwards in Milledgeville), Alice down the road in Eatonton, and myself, if I may join them for a moment, in Fitzgerald, reaching out and joining hands around a small area where women have lived vibrant, intense lives for hundreds of years without reaching for the pen.

Writers now, women especially, have come to be grown in the time of the great sexual wars. To be, and in which order, writer, woman, Southern: work is always cut out for me. The worn question is never asked much in the South— what do women want. A pity, since the equivocation of a handful of Viennese women years ago has had to do. If only

Sigmund had asked my blind grandmother she would have blasted his expectations. What do women want? Sigmund, ask me the next question, because first of all I get edgy when I'm limited to categories, whether it's white, biped, female, hard-headed (the most common adjective applied to me when I was a child), doefooted, tongue-tied or gifted. And all I want is to converse at least twice a week with someone under ten years old. I want that ground corn meal soap from England. In the South, home of more stereotypes *per capita* than any place in the U.S., I want a language adequate to the experience. I want organic produce, and not those over-sized hothouse strawberries. Hard work, the French language for relief, someone who does not hedge love, stinted love being the most killing characteristic in the round world. It's far better to be alone with a stack of travel books and a quilt Granny made than sleep with someone who has ye olde English property rights stamped on his chromosomes; that view is a dog and cat idea of the world. I want change, and rib-aching laughter, and to go to Lascaux. I want my past; it's tragic and amusing.

From my perspective, the perspective of the keyhole, the runaway, the good girl, and the exile, the long line of people and traditions I am of and against are as much a great dump as they are rich and yielding to me. The tension of the Southern culture within the U.S. and the tightening of that tension because of being female, tunes my pitch. I do sift that compost heap. My muse is part goat, swallowing can after can. The past charges very day with its alternating or direct current. As a result, I never can separate cause and effect, even though my linear logical brain works better than it should. As a child I stomped and said, But we don't have to say ALL that, we can skip over to the end. The talk looped and meandered like old rivers. I want this: a discontinuous present in my style. Sometimes a cloudy syntax. It suits my sense of the blue wave that carries events forward. I was furious often as a child when the only answer I got was, Because I said so. As a writer, that satisfies. I had too the gift of numbers. Often I knew the answer without the figuring, a quality of many idiots, I was told when I leapt over some minor calculation with a bill or cubic footage. That process, unexplainable, has everything to do with the taproots of writing. It lets me say here that I live now in San Francisco. Last week, someone visiting me for the first time walked in, looked around slowly, and in a guarded voice said, "This is aggressively feminine."

I was raised by a network of women, a world as private as purdah. Among themselves, my mother's friends were brutally frank, raucous, and never oblivious to compromise. They went out as if disguised by veils. Appearance. And innocence, the vise that keeps women "girls" well into their sixties. A generality may have a use, as does a bludgeon, but it obliterates what is of particular use by oversimplifying. Nothing has been dealt this blow so much as the Southern woman, black and white. The power behind the throne, iron hand in velvet glove, she endured (what else could she do), belle of three counties, a little vixen, a great lady, *ad infinitum*, and all evidence to the contrary notwithstanding. The splendid matriarchs with power in the open are rare birds. And always endangered. More common is the third rate power, manipulation. We learned it as we learned cartwheels and the multiplication table. I had my daddy wrapped around my little finger when I was five because I was the prettiest little thing, etc. We firmly believed Scarlet would have to get Rhett back. For what we have come to call "role models" of independent living, there were just the old maid ticket takers at the theatre, the librarian with the gray bun, and the McCall sisters who looked like twin bulldogs and taught first and third grades. You must suffer for beauty, the beaten down mother will say as she curls her daughter's hair so tight that her eyes are drawn sideways. You'll end up like *that*. Your brains are showing, she says, as she goes under for the third time. You'll have teaching to fall back on, she says later. I was a little devil being raised to be a lady. Much of it took, like a big vaccination scab leaving me well-marked. Where Freud, causality, linearity break down is that I was not convinced; and the training was rigorous. The aunt who looked like a witch told me over and over that she had to gather her twenty beaux to the front porch of Daddy Jack's house to announce her selection of the one to marry. I'd glance over at Wilfred, *numero uno*, with the enormous wart on the side of his nose, as he nodded over the Sunday paper. At an early age, I caught on to the fantasy world. Appearance. A box with a false bottom. A black rag doll who turns into a white doll when I turned her upside down. The green soft moss I jumped on behind the cotton mill and found out it was the sewage. My father in his white suit fished me out shouting curses. Almost everything is more plural than it seems. Perhaps I was influenced by having naturally curly hair that never had to be mangled into shape. I missed the litanies of the beauty parlor. And when I heard "to fall back on," I imagined instead, falling backwards into the Oconee from the side of a rowboat and floating off. Such are protections. I never slept well and so acquired the habit of reading several books a week. But that's standard procedure for a writer. That, and I had an encouraging teacher, flask in lower right hand desk drawer, who said only, Go far away to school, as far away as possible.

Notwithstanding was a word my mother and hers used often. An archaic word which expressed a day to day philosophy. It was rather like the artist sent on the expedition to the New World in the 17th century. He was commissioned to draw the great virgin forests. Since he never had seen any trees but the pollarded plane trees in the parks of Paris, he came home with stacks of sketches of those, never drawing a leaf or limb of the American forests.

And writing, notwithstanding the program: decadence, the old bigots, the whispered racial slurs, the bores, the family album of alcoholics, old aunts propped in chairs saying only "da-da," the slow motion suicides. These *are* the givens of the moss-draped South in general, and of my family in particular. These are the terms of the lease, and still the rent is due every month. This is endless subject matter to avoid or explore. I think of Flannery O'Connor's subjects, that taut line she walked between raising questions and answering them, and how she landed time after time just on the side of the widest possiblity. Her eye was too accurate to simplify. She knew there are no Southerners, no theoretical models, only a family resemblance you sometimes spot, stopped at a redlight, that makes you press the accelerator hard. I didn't like to go near my blind grandmother whose eyeballs were blank as hailstones because she wanted to feel my hair, feel the ends of my fingernails, touch my clothes to see if the seams were "Frenched." She never asked how school was. I admire that kind of writing.

I remember the women of my family who laid swatches of fabric over sofas, who had always, samples of peach, ivory, teal, and cream paint in their purses, who contemplated the recovered wing chair with the attention surgeons give to incisions. The act of attention was intense and disciplined. The *place* must have a sense of itself. Greens and blues will fool you, you don't remember shades as well as you think. I want the color and polish and devotion in my lines. I want the windows clean. Pellucid: admitting the maximum passage of light. If the house is a metaphor, it is also totally real. Fabric, stitching, tatting, piecing into designs, interfacing for durability and form, making patterns out of newspaper. I like the methods; I hem words by picking up the stitch, doubling back for it then going forward, around a circle. Writing, the bright words, the tension of the seam.

We were fabric people, as others are the Miwok people, circus people, lost people. Texture. My hand rises too naturally; the museum guard senses me immediately as I circle the sculpture. His eye is sharply on me. I run my hand over the poem. In the cotton mill, my father's business, the light is gray because cotton lint catches in the screened windows. Oily black machines, gigantic looms strung, beautiful as harps, the shuttles pulled by women in faded soft dresses. Bins to climb, dive into piled raw cotton. In the tin cup of the scale over the bin, I ride, the needle jerking between 60-65 pounds, to fly out, the landing not as gentle as I would want. But to fly, actually, as in dreams. A natural act, as later I would swing out over the spring on vines at night, dropping into cold black water below, crawl up the slippery bank, grabbing roots, then swinging out again and again for that moment of falling. Water moccasins, thick as my leg, thirty pound rockfish with primitive snouts, even crocodiles lived in these streams with "boils," the deep sources of icy water I dove for, pushing my fist into the bubbling force at the bottom of the stream.

Do I write like a Southerner? Do I write like a woman? There really can be no *like*, since my situation in both cases is not figurative, but literal. I'm after discovering my place as a writer on my own. This is partly out of preference, but if it were not out of preference it would be out of necessity. As Southern, woman and writer, as with blacks and others, I'm not usually included in the canon. Of the dozens of histories of twentieth century literature I have read, not one connects to my whole sense of poetry or fiction. I'm fascinated when I fall into an article which poses a rhetorical question then proceeds to answer, give the final word with a series of supporting cases, ignoring the hundreds of others. "Is Literature Always Reactionary?" for instance. Glad I asked? From the outside, there is the Tradition, which swallows whole the Individual Talent, and there is the distaff tradition, the bands of marauders and true believers taking pot shots or haranguing the laurel crown boys. Two sit-coms.

What the dead-eye traditionalists and the *avant-garde* have in common is a self-referential world of purely literary cross-pollination. This is a vast subject and it has hardly been touched, ever. This morning I read an essay on the connection of poetic structure to the mathematical concept of a closed field. I felt as if I were reading the directions to a board game. Later, my dog died. I was holding her in my lap. I need more inclusive theories. If the *garde* is galloping on and on through academe, equating the rhythm of their hooves to moral order, while the new theorists thrust banners *avant*, and *bord`a bord*, or *derrière* this is all very interesting. Theoretically. With the kindest will in the world, I feel stifled. And after literary history, after all of criticism, there is history itself, that infinite logical fallacy rolling on and on without noticing custom, birth, food, nature. History has chosen wars and treaties. Why not the symbolism of lilacs, why not?

Therefore, I feel a secret quality to my writing. Many women do. Make do. A wonderful pair of verbs together, primitive as hoecake. My sense of form starts not with loose iambs, or rebellion against structuralism, but with an instinct for transference. I like the skeletons of fish, the rhythm of windshield washers, the sonar photo of a fetus which looks like a galaxy. The putting up of peach pickles is as clear a method as the structure of a sestina. The good stead of pretend rooms under tableclothes and stairs, an artisitc space which lived vividly for an afternoon.

While my father ran the mill, hunted, my mother gathered,

made perfect luncheons, with the aid of our cook Willie Bell, and our house pulsated with cleanliness. My clothes came from Macon. We went to the beach in the summer for a month. Fitzgerald was as rigidly hierarchical as the English aristocracy, with dukes, and bar sinisters, local duchesses in black Cadillacs, many earls, and, of course, ladies, ladies, ladies. My family, with no claims on education, sophistication, or *noblesse oblige*, was upper crust. Everything had a place and everything was in it. I stepped out of my underpants on the floor and they were in my drawer, pressed, the next morning. It was a cloying and obnoxious world, but I was in it and was nothing if not secure in my rung. Even the town was ordered, one of the few planned towns in the country. Dispossessed veterans from North and South gathered there after the War between the States and devised a perfect grid one mile square. The streets are straight as cannon shot. Those running east and west are named after Southern trees: Jessamine, Lemon, Pine, Magnolia; north and south running streets are reminders of the war: Lee, Grant, Sherman, and the four borders are battleships: Monitor, Merrimac, Roanoke, Sultana. The lack of curves is relieved by broad streets with islands of palms, azaleas and gardenias. Thirty feet of amaryllis my mother planted when I was small still bloom on the island across from the Methodist Church. As in most Southern towns, the black people lived all around. So near and so far. When my grandfather was mayor he named the town "The Colony City." Like other colonies, the news seemed distant.

Until I went to college, I never had seen a real bookstore. Our literature was mail order. We had Book of the Month. We subscribed to *Harper's Bazaar*, which seemed like photos from another planet, *Reader's Digest* (slow), and *Arizona Highways*, for some reason. News, politics: never discussed. Ideas: no one had any worth mentioning. Talk was of *should*, of standards, local gossip. Years after, my new husband and I drove home from Stanford in the VW. Martin Luther King had just been murdered. "Let's not discuss it," my uncle said, "He had it coming." Last word. An air of profound criticism, really, at bottom, a deep hopelessness toward life and all its manifestations.

The great exception to that is hospitality. To be a woman is to cook like the devil. There's the *jouissance*, that fine forgotten-in-English word. Food is the biggest metaphor of all. I pull the poem out of the typewriter and see if it's simmering or at the rolling boil. Pressed chicken, brown sugar muffins, quail (smothered), grits with cheese, a spectrum of pies with lemon meringue as the lowest, and black bottom pie as the epitome. Lane cake which no Northerner could ever hope to emulate in this life or the next, and key lime when Mr. Bernhardt got in the Key West limes. No matter what. Unconditionally, we will cook, from restorative broths to the great heroic meals. A craft, a philosophy much more evolved than nuclear warheads.

The under belly of growing up in that relatively privileged, ill-starred society, was that my family was unable to figure out how to live. My parents, beautiful physically, fought and tore each other up. Every day was chaos. Shouting and slamming doors and roaring off in the car in the middle of the night. I had to oil my feathers constantly to keep it all sliding off. Years from then, I learned the psychoanalytic terms that fit my parents like mint in the julep. They were truly wild, an unliterary Scott and Zelda, ruined by the Depression, the hope just pulled out from under them so that they never trusted anything. Nothing in our family festered; we shouted, threw cups. When I was five, a mill employee shot my father in the side. He'd aimed for my grandfather and my father heroically stepped in front and was wounded. Two other people in the office were killed and the murderer eventually went to the electric chair, his death witnessed by many people in town. From kindergarten through high school, the murderer's daughter was in my class. We played together at recess. The South is a double whammy; my family a triple threat. Flannery and Carson could make mincemeat out of them. "Please, don't ever write a novel," my sister begs. "Let sleeping dogs lie." Yes, just let them wake up on the old country porch now and then to thump their tails.

When a reviewer complained of my "far out imaginings," I read my poems again, trying to understand. Octavio Paz said of Mexico that surrealism runs in the streets . That is, there is no such thing, except from an outside point of view. Like Latin Americans, we Southerners who write, naturally write from a culture that still throws out unexpected events and images from its core. Why do Southerners write about freaks, someone asked Flannery. "It is because we are still able to recognize one," she snapped.

Certain other advantages stay clear. With mothers and aunts whispering for generations, *We feel sorry for men*, I spared myself the long argument with Freud, who, I sensed, never listened to the dream itself anyway. At thirteen, in the Carnegie Library, where I was told if a book was not "suitable," I found the Great Books, untouched on a top shelf, a long row in gray buckram. The fist one I read, in the middle of Mazo de la Roche and Yerby, was INTERPRETATION OF DREAMS. Even then, I thought, out of the fullness of ignorance, this man has the wrong idea. One thing I know for sure is that I never envied the penis of anyone, and neither did any woman in Ben Hill County. And *my* dreams, so clear and whole did not want interpretation; they *were*, and were much more interesting as themselves: unlimited images.

To be a woman is to own nightgowns softer than blossoms in a peach blow. Beneath the vocabulary there's the muscle of the language. Beneath the batiste and the trim of eyelet and smocking is the smear of blood, armpits smelling of dry herbs and resin, a feather of hair, the sex like a Japanese garden of 100 mosses in the dark. Is to know the rooster foot is good for thickening, the cooter foot is good in soup. If you scald claws until tough skin and talons slip off, then you've got something. Has anyone ever told you these things? Aggressively feminine, as the man said. I would not have thought to put it quite that way, but it will do.

Listening to women— playing bridge, shelling peas, visiting the dressmaker, those who were dead seemed present. Lively in memory, a way time fans out. Listening from just out of sight, I could imagine the person evoked to be rounding the corner, about to call out, instead of staring up for many years at the underside of a coffin lid made by the Brothers Paulk. Talk, talk. Language. Words as tactile as pebbles and bits of broken glass. Georgia has a fine enunciated , lyrical gentry speech, a chopped-bedrock hillbilly speech, and the syrup rich deep black speech, with good stories to hear from all. To hear vowels like musical notes, translate sound into rivers, wings, rain. I want dictionaries always, and etymology texts, and foreign voices passing under the window. The connection I feel with all speech, all words seems endless, though the beginnings are finite: an ancient black babysitter telling me stories about the "brownies," who could fly to Africa. "Now you're a brownie," she would say, "you just don't know it." Her smoky whites of eyes and little white tufts of hair standing out in the dim bedtime light. "You go to sleep, Brownie, or the brownies will take you off." The other source was the tubercular doctor next door who sat me on his bony knees and told me of an eagle who took off curly headed babies. A soaring eagle, he gestured, meanwhile spitting brown juices that spattered on my legs. I was afraid of catching TB and even then was too polite to wipe off my leg. He was the eagle, craggy, old yellowed eyes, a big suit he seemed to flap around in.

In fifth grade, we learned poems. By heart. That summer, jammed with my mother, sisters, and Willie Bell, along with a month's supply of clothes, games, and junk in the car, we crossed the rickety bridge from Brunswick to St. Simon's Island, and I saw the marsh grasses waving, sensed suddenly the land not earth, not water, but both, with the grass moving in time with the tide, the sulphur wind, the Spanish moss. Then it came to mind, by heart:

> As the marsh-hen secretly builds on the watery sod,
> Behold I will build me a nest on the greatness of God:
> I will fly in the greatness of God as the marsh-hen flies
> In the freedom that fills all the space 'twixt the marsh
> and the skies....

The jolt of connection. "Look-- the Marshes of Glenn. We had a poem about them," I shouted. No one seemed impressed. After that, I had a new sense, like taste and smell. Uninterrupted "poetic time," as Blake called it, was over. Poetic time: to float naked for a mile, bathing suit tied to my ankle for the return upstream. Poetic time: to hunt arrowheads after rain when they stand up on the eroded clay. To pick up flint, the stone feeling like the word, and bits of pottery painted in zigzags of black, a mixture of soot and ashes. Poetic time: the moment between when the chicken's head is snappped off and when it flops over. Running in a crazy circle. To write now is not to recount experience, but to tap into time, pull out a core sample.

Memory is capricious. Who knows what influences are. Rather remember that over thousands of years the microscopic skeletons of radiolaria fused and formed the cliffs of Dover. Layers and layers. When I open a powdery, mildewed book, I'm catapulated by the smell to the back hallway of my grandparents' house. I play an ancient wind-up record; K-K-K Katy crackles in my ear. Through mullioned panes, my grandmother's bedroom: chintz, hatboxes, lavender. And another smell of chicken with too much pepper. Faces, objects, smells, landscapes-- all open up like an Advent calendar, full of secret doors.

What is stunning is how little is remembered. I would like to have the silent areas of my cortex stimulated to regain the lost links. In memory too, cause and effect break apart. Bergson is right; if the industrial revolution had not happened, we could find logical ABC reasons to explain whatever happened instead. I could trace the threads leading me right now to the Peace Corps in Africa, to the country club in Moultrie, Georgia, or to the radio station, WGHB in Fitzgerald, where the Story Lady read every evening to the children in the core of the core of Dixie. All possible lives. But in actual choices, made one by one, I came to the fantasy of myself writing books, living in a beautiful city, and miraculously, this is the present reality.

STIRRING A BLACK BEAN SOUP FOR FERNANDO

Good herbs go in the pot,
the incense of the clay gods
of Nicaragua rising over our heads.
We must solve memory, the dancing
at night under *palapa,* I touched
in all that movement only his hand
and fine cotton shoulder. He made
the marimba go slow like music
beating on our ribs. We'll always
leave that country. The shadow
of the guard walks across the shutters.
Who is out there, parting
the heavy air? Slow simmer,
the ladle pulls up gristle. This
is momentary. We look in the eye
of the bone. The guns came out
of every house. The Sandinista
whispers: it is thrilling to kill
the uniform. But like moonflowers
that bloom only for the dark,
we forfeit fear. Lay the plates,
mash the black beans to a pulp.
He made a lovely explosion.
A fact as simple as a spoon.
Cloves and bay. Opaque swirls.
But we are so intelligent.
We go backwards and forwards.
We always leave a mark in the book,
the wrong book.

SONG OF THE GULLAH

Salt marsh, a pull of tide
in grasses waving. Here,
some waded into the surf,
here, flew home to Africa, and
after that we always could fly
from one world to the other.

In the huts of the past,
louder than this, cast
iron pots took in the noise
of magic. We dreamed
in ceremonial slowness,
like a flapping of large
wings. Now, we're out
of narrow holds. Out
of nets thrown over
our backs on the beach.
Sea biscuits and no
language, and then
outline of a coast
forever negative. Sense
of limitless struggle
as part of our skin.

At heart, the jungle, veld,
lions, have no scapes or
faces here. But in clouds
when we drifted, drifted
to the far grasses on
the other side, all chants
took on the voice of flies
in a wound. In the thick
air we could move nowhere.

To learn to slash cane
chop cotton beat rice down.
To walk the crop rows at night
carrying a candle to talk
back to the moon. Drawing
in black dirt and our songs
blending over years with
white Christ's. The English
foot taking a step into
our dancing, their waltz and turn.

The land is strangely
good along the coast.
In other words, we looked
for similarities and
found fine sand, wild
rose and plum, she-crabs,
the great plate of sun
serving all. We crossed
countless thresholds,
pushed our tongues against
our teeth to make new
sounds, wasted our dreams
in the heat, waiting.

We were animal life
discounted from reality.
The skin of a Gullah
shines like a blue bead.
Skin oiled like rich
wood from the forests
we were sucked out of
on the last days
of the reign of the gods.

Our lives were pulled
shallow as peanut plants
from the ground and
left to dry in the other
tropic. We were gourds
hung up in the trees
for anyone's nests.

The new lord never listened.
Gullah is spoken low.
When we sang only
the palms heard us. Only
the foxes repected
our pain. Only the sand
soaked us in. This is where
we waded into the waters,
this is why we fly.

LOOKING FOR WILLIE BELL

If I thought this the bright large season,
well the taxi is lost. Greasy streets
squeezing by the ruins. Among the detritus
of the wrecking ball, few red and green
lights. We won't ask the wino curled on
a stoop. Brake only for the shattering of sheets
of smoked glass. In this tract, life
is eternal. Iced over potholes. We pick

A way among the lost. I look for one of them.
She's Newark now. Scrap of address
is a corner store quiescent with boredom,
the cashier waiting to be taken in the dark
boundary of crime. She's nowhere, only
somewhere, with a memory of land her only
sweetness: shampooing her hair with rain
from tornadoes, the cotton crop would just come,
barking of yard dogs in swirls of red dust.
When her husband called her fool
that was the end of as she knew it.
Urban wrecks, misfires, blood. Which

Stained face in the streetlight is hers?
The gray takes away all blue, except sparks
of fire on the sawtooth horizon of Manhattan.
Enough blows to the eyes: there's a halo
around the bombsite. I thought I'd find
her tonight. Sullen festival of lights.
Surprising in the swerve— the moon,
as on the rim of the world. Instant
beauty of silvered curb, colored
shadows of tenements. She's somewhere.

Around the smudgepots squat bodies
in vacant lots can not discuss candlelight
reflected in the white glass of
The Swedenborgs, like sun from under water,
do not discuss the light in each others'
eyes. They pace up and down, wading
through torn grasses and I push the lock
down, look right and left, sideways.

OCTOBER: SLASH AND BURN

Great moon suffused with blood.
Hours move in front of me like
a stitchripper in a tight seam.
I think of the suicide of the blind
man who was suddenly able to see.
His white stick numb, his peeled
eyes aching on their dark side.
Hunter's moon, slash and burn.

This night is perfection.
The moon lights up fast animals
in the stubble, as in the time
when the scarecrow wore a silk
hat and if we followed the hounds
from find to death, our faces
were marked with fox blood.

No one can eat or die or take
a bath for you. Time to plant
cuttings of the flowering
Yesterday, Today, Tomorrow,
the hair-roots committed
to creamy petals, fragrance
for the summer shade. Vera saw
a Japanese man buried in ice.
As she told me, she was twisting
her Persian necklace. The sun
picked out hairline cracks
around her eyes. I think of her.

The name Vera means faith and
we will be following her a long time
across vast fields to the serrated
crevasse, boom of avalanche higher up.

Today, driving through the underpass,
a gull swooped down just as the train
approached and the blast of the whistle
came whole out of the gull's throat.

In my vision, the dangling rope
twists. Her jacket a scarlet wing
splayed. I hunt and gather.
Jackrabbits freeze when moonlight
glints blue on the double barrel.
Caroline King is old as a field.
She came into memory on an Indian pony,
her hair red fire.
Fluid is swirling around her heart.
For 98 years she got what she made.
She says goodbye solidly, thanks
us for being on earth when she was.

Her bread knife cuts deep in time.
The earth is open.
Campanula, foxglove, ranunculus,
paper narcissus, and the beautiful
walking lilies. I'll slip them
in the crack between two worlds.

INTO THIS VIEW

Comes autumn. The clouds are bleached, trees pollarded.
The city has no gingko street, and no memory of mine

Ever happened here in fall. Always the season wants home.
I attempt a new relationship with sky. I read Heraclitus

And look out, level with clouds forming and disbanding.
There flagrant maples blocked the middle distance.

Now, fog, cuffing every window, foghorns all night. Him
I used to sleep by ground his teeth as if not to call out

With this soft, water voice. The woman downstairs cries
as I read Wittgenstein. Her sobs in the floor feel

Like a stone drum. And what does this really mean?
Her name is Susan. I remember many of them by now.

By now. Where's that? Headlights top the hill and go
over. If there's a nightingale, darkling, let it fly.

When I leave the city it is to slip out of a white envelope.
Elsewhere, autumn is as I know it.

THE SHADOW OF INCREASE

Something of yours as charm
I'm wanting. You, when you could
have turned toward some openwork
folk motif of hearts, said:
Henceforth from the mind.

I see you striding down Third
on payday, carrying your treat
of jasmine soap wrapped in rice paper
and a pint of bourbon for the long Sunday.

When I cross into your mind
with its matching geometric borders
made of shards, the lock clicks
behind each page. Louise,
you make no sound now. Water

In the estuaries still flashes
silver as the sand takes it, and
rivulets slide over the porous rocks
with no denial. Tonight the sky
was a hundred colors and it did darken.

Your capable hands are unstrapping
the steel band around my chest.
Words move on this tongue:
work the wind has to do, shaping the pines,
the natural crush the foot makes
through the crisp rime of ice.
I want to do as you did not,
for all the wilderness in us.
Under the great balanced day,
the world is pilfering me for joy.
Your words float across the whitest silence.

for Louise Bogan

TO SHINE

When I have no glow I keep writing to the colony of pale lepers.
Silver backs of mirrors deepen as toward the underworld.

I leave marks, white flake initials on the birch, shimmer
of genuine scar tissue. My knifeblade, quick as an eyelid closing,

scrapes granite with sparks of song. The swirl under the bridge
swallows my face. As if only for emphasis, the beacon picks out

phosphorous from fulgent swells. I beckon to bandoleers, to
flamingoes wintering over in my waters. In fantasy, all is

epiphany: in a window next door, a bald man with incandescent
head, and above, a woman in gold blushing over a glass of phlox,

ribbons of fragrance rising around her. But all actual light
is the candle in each eye of my greyhound. Real life has no

form and floats the distance like ambergris. With the western
sky so bleak, I have to move to the Argentine. I want to walk

boulevards lined with banners, the wide doorways with diaphanous
curtains various colors of pearl. It is time for other phenomenon,

other teacups, blind alleys with a gloss of rain. There is no
blemish on my dreams; they reach to the ancient festival of brightfire.

I step quickly, start to weave, throw, braid. To be candid,
to catch the flashing bream. Why not clarity, why not.

A photo of white clay cliffs, a handkerchief in a bowl
of bluing offer examples. It's apparent, the eyeballs of that

porcelain doll expect to radiate, and the gelding's silver bridle,
scintillating, when I push him through the sun. In the black

inside a walnut, there's a needlepoint of light. I'm kindling the
divine. Smoky berries, caviar of beluga, blanc-mange, a cold éclair.

PAUSE. PREHISTORIC

In the dry Dordogne in the heat I pause,
rub my body with oil, and head for the cave
with spotted horses on the wall.
40,000 years. I've come this far:
stony lanes to swerve down, the walnut forest's
leaves edged with bronze light. If now
you expect words like coins of the realm,
practical as metabolism, well, I fogot
them too. I'm layers down from there,

Closer to the memory that "barbarian"
was onomatopoeic Greek for the voices
of invaders-from-without. Disquieting:
handprints on limestone. Louder than
language. When you were the quiet one,
I was constantly, constantly asking,
Life? Life? Turgid questions moving
like shears over wet sheep. From this

Great silence, I'd like to wave
back to the painter of horses. So much
nearer than your fine laugh. What's
good too in Dordogne is the house of La Boëtie,
standing in the square in Sarlat. His friend,

Asked where the love between them came from,
answered, "Because it was I, because it was he."
The cave artists must have been cold.
I don't touch the hump on the wall where one
painted the swell of the bull's chest.
The sure stroke of realism, and the rest
is brilliance and old air. "I was in my life
alone," Frost said, never travelling out.
I can stand hours, invisible, thinking

the thoughts of all travellers before me,
feel the same feather along my spine.
The animals are singular and

Blaze out of time whole and present.
I think of your pleasure, the glint
of light on your teeth in the dark.
So much continues to acquiesce,
but each horse refuses. I like the vigor
of black outline, gold on pale stone,
rose-madder, the blood-sticky red
against rough gray. The way I go
on is in answer to the question

How? I've eaten a peck of salt with no
one here. When Mansfield died, Woolf
told her diary she'd keep writing, "but
into emptiness." Do you know I'm writig
this wet from the shower, sitting on
the edge of a little wicker stool.
The cave animals seem to have bioluminescence,
that charge I feel hidden in my black
marrow. I'm not waiting for anything.
My skin, holding the heat: I'm writing
you the word: immortal.

DECEMBER, THUNDER IS IN THE MIDDLE OF EARTH

In the circle of this year
I am what is around me.
The bees wake and hum a symphony of praise.
I tickle my dead grandmother's face with a blade of grass.
Sweet water in wells will heal you.
Begin the spellbinding:
a year like no other

And it will not ever be over.
Never the infant Jesus for me
or the kneeling oxen at that hour, but
it is the African night rich with stars and the travellers
setting out with three words in hammered casks.
So much comes too late.
What to do now with the silver skates
and a red skirt to whirl in when you spin
on the brittle ice under no moon.
When you are devouring your prey
nothing can reach you.

At midnight the animals will speak English.
The love will fit.
You stir the banked coals in the kitchen, throw on the seasoned
oak. The feast, the earth turning back, gifts
still unopened. Ribbons stream back from the dog
racing through the house wild with joy wild
with invincible ignorance. We were serious
now we can laugh. Jupiter and Saturn will conjunct
and blaze as the houses darken. In the copse
of empty trees the hounds run down the speared boar.
Take it limb by limb.

Pull in the plumb line.
We throw a stone
in the circle of this year.

A QUIPU KNOT FOR ARGUEDAS

You play slow chess in the cold
plaza, hands balled in your pockets
except to make a move. The Indians
sell soft oranges, rugs, and wait,
who knows, for the return of Inca Rey,
born yesterday and already walking
across the pampa of Anta to Cuzco.
The hardest light in the hemisphere
hits this place. Darkness
still flows from the stones, Arguedas.
You first arrived with your papa
at night, touched the Incan wall
undulating and unpredictable as a river.
The stones are alive; lines you touched
burned the palms of your hand.
You push the queen around my travelling
magnetic board. The sun rims the plaza.
Cuzco: navel. The power pulls your insides.

When the Maria Angola tolls, the bells
vibrate in your teeth, the bells
cast with Incan gold, with human fat,
resonate in the bones of your back.
Because of them, no need to tell
a story, when reality is cold enough.
The bells lower and lower the silence.
Ringing that filled your body as a child,
burst from your throat. I watch
your brown hand on the pawn.
When a boy points at me, you laugh.
I'm closed out of Quechua, syllables
of hashed rock. Light eyes, cat eyes
the boy called me. My skin blooms
tourist like an itch. I have an ear

for the reedy music, somewhere
the same chords I can't touch.
Like the Spanish adobe, each tremor
shakes off that *fol de rol* and more
tight rock is revealed. When the sun
shines on them they seem to glisten
like blood. You are fluid, swarm
with those opposing currents. The place,
something too hurt, too old.

The women will wait it out.
Always they wind in wool.
You watch one place her five potatoes
in a circle. Her cheeks suck in.
Light polishes the skins to gold.
You know the stones will never be warm.
The bite at the heart of fruit
when you have no fruit. What's the logic?
You turn your face to the sun.
I feel my ribs aching against my chest.
No air, hard to breathe. I open
the corn wrapped in husks like a little
doll made to accompany the dead. Peppery,
steaming. I eat off my hand,
leaf through DEEP RIVERS. Your words
go out in cold whorls. I see
that whistling top you learned to spin
as a boy, its leaps and sound of wings,
turning smoothly as water around rock.
The wooden sphere with a burned nail
for axis. The same string starts
your book, the core, the widening circles.
I blow on my fingers. You're warmer
in your shoes made of water.

It took two hundred Incas to dance
the gold chain around the plaza,
the links thick as wrists.

You've stomped your feet, you
in old leggings and poncho worn
to threads. Your time went by
singed between fire and love.
I can get close enough to feel
your body's warmth. Remember,
I'm travelling. I read, drink *chicha*
in little bars, listen to *huaynos.*
Your eyes, Arguedas, the sun melts
just there. A blue fly lights
on your arm I would go
on the Santa Ana train with you tomorrow,
daypacks to Ollantaytambo, the Incan
road, the Urubamba down the gorge
flashing like the lost chain.
But four Indians already have carried
your box through the street
following the mestizo in black
who played on a crude violin, what music.